Shadrach and Other Poems

Oka Obono

Langaa Research & Publishing CIG
Mankon, Bamenda

Publisher:
Langaa RPCIG
Langaa Research & Publishing Common Initiative Group
P.O. Box 902 Mankon
Bamenda
North West Region
Cameroon
Langaagrp@gmail.com
www.langaa-rpcig.net

Distributed in and outside N. America by African Books Collective
orders@africanbookscollective.com
www.africanbookcollective.com

ISBN: 9956-717-17-7

© *Oka Obono 2011*

Dedicated to the Shadrach things in life and my wife, Koblowe, who helps me understand them.

Contents

Dedication
Foreword
Preface

Foreword

It is true that those with very fertile imagination are not necessarily found only in departments of literary studies. They do not have to possess degrees in disciplines devoted to teaching the craft of writing. The best of creative writing sometimes comes from individuals whose professions are very distant from imaginative writing and rhetoric. Indeed, one of the challenges of our postmodern condition is that all provinces of knowledge have to cross pollinate or interact to enrich one another. In this regard, the philosophical and sociological application of creative writing becomes something more than a mere attempt by a writer to pass comments in order not to be seen as writing what has no immediate social relevance.

At a time when critics of Nigerian literature are expressing concern over the declining quality of creative writing in the country, Oka Obono, sociologist by training, comes into the troubled scene with *Shadrach and Other Poems*, a collection of poems that anyone could easily mistake as having been written by Wole Soyinka or other celebrated masters of the Word. Densely philosophical and challengingly taut in language, the Shadrach poems engage the audience in a voyage through pleasurable agony, asking how possible it is to travel light when one's heart is heavy; wishing it were possible to skip tomorrows and their blows.

The poet-protagonist may be a sufferer, but is also one in whom we read ourselves in our struggles with being and becoming. As he agonizes over finding the self writing "at a bad time" when what he sees are "faces of disgraces," we become more and more aware of the other meaning of "Shadrach" as our own social and cultural failures. Human suffering is partly created by society and may, unfortunately, be made a way of life. Thus, being thrown into society by accident of birth or other circumstance is already one variable that underlies the fact that "Dogs were born free.../And everywhere/They are in chains," a thoughtful parody of the philosophical dictum that "Man is born free but everywhere he is in chains."

Dogs will not always remain in chains, as the recent experiences of populations rising to oust their governments in the Arab countries of North Africa have shown. It is not dogs that are now afraid of their supposed owners who have for long kept them on the leash. Rather it is the supposed owners that are now afraid of the dogs. "Beware of dogs" as a warning speech act does not exclude the owner of the dog as its audience, even though we assume that every dog knows and will always submit to its owner.

Shadrach, a telling image of trial, is about a journey through the furnace: "An inferno so steep it was no ordinary fire." The furnace of our trials also purifies. Ordinarily, it seems designed to consume, but it also refines and makes ready. Those who have no eyes to look through the inferno cannot see this difference that emerges and merges the beginning with the end, the tragic with the heroic triumph.

The Word will never die: it rises out of the ashes like the phoenix. The poems in this collection are the heroes of the fight between Light and Darkness. The poems have not just survived and triumphed over the furnace, they have also tamed the furnace.

Reading the poems in this enthralling collection is also an encounter with the refining power of the best language of the best of arts. In the poems one finds the spark, the crackle, the rage, and the glow of the finest imagination. Reading the poems means having a rewarding experience with creative fire: it is like making the mythical trip to the grove of the gods to borrow fire with which to begin a new technology.

With this collection that is characterized by a highly impressive stylistic vigour, Oka Obono has taken his place among the best voices in African poetry of the century. It is a collection that will, for a long time, be talked about for its depth of imagination and for the profundity of its philosophical exploration of personal and social experience.

Obododimma Oha
Associate Professor of Cultural Semiotics and Stylistics
Department of English
University of Ibadan, Nigeria.
13 February 2011

Preface

On the morning of Thursday, 24 November 2005, fire broke out in my Sociology Department office at the University of Ibadan. Nothing was saved except a file containing scraps of paper on which I had written these poems over the preceding two decades. Mostly written by 1995, the poems constituted an emotional biography, or a loose personal chronicle of arbitrary events and contemplations occurring in what proved to be the fieriest periods of my life up to that point.

Today, they remain germane to readings of transitions that subsequently took place by providing a background of burdens borne through what I can only now describe as a furnace of aspiration. But I never lost my ambivalence toward them. Some were products of deep inner excoriations, meant for my eyes only. The poems were never intended for public consumption.

The fire changed that. It altered my perceptions of the world and the reason for human ordeals. I saw existence as one complex fire. We are baked dark in it. Yet, it is through its furnaces that dross is eliminated and we obtain clearer insights into the questions of purpose, courage, power and destiny. I realized that, like I, the poems had passed through an ontological crucible. The Shadrach idea became my choice of a redeeming metaphor that indicated the triumph of the human spirit over temporal setbacks and its indictment of forces falsely proclaiming their permanence.

I owe immense gratitude to Tade Ipadeola, Benson Eluma, Carla Cherry and Usani Obono for conversations leading to the publication of these poems; Lindiwe Makubalo for her thoughts on the marginal Abednego;

ix

and Obododimma Oha for writing such a humbling foreword to the collection. As Koblowe put it, he was "the right writer" for this purpose. I salute all those who, passing through one Shadrach moment or the other, however seemingly ruinous, know in advance it is temporary. It is not any more destructive than the creative visions such moments can give rise to.

Oka Obono
Ibadan
4 April 2011

Preludes

On the road again,
A silly raindrop splashes
Smack on my nose
Flattening it some more.
It elates me
It deflates me.

But I cannot see the great connection between
Raindrops and noses –
Cannot understand why that raindrop was . . .
        So happy.

The squelch is in my moccasins.
I must remove my soul from my feet
Lest she slip
Away and stare at me
From the glistening pond
The true mirror of my age.

Distant Images

Standing here on this cliff of change
I survey
The grand landmass
The tumbling hills and rolling waters
Pondering what bird that is
By the shoreline.

Asaba

Asaba sleeps early
We roar untired
Into the night swiftly
Alabaman marauders raiding
The innocence of the still, silent night.

On the banks of that Niger
We roar all night
These tigers and I
Finding succour in the sounds which surround us
It is a fitting time to die.

On the streets a vagrant spectacle appears
A prancing peacock
Pees in a gulley
Muttering
Tottering
Rapidly following after
As though to say
He should not let himself go that way. . .

Till Asaba stirs awake
A demure maiden
Casually lifting
The foggy veil which covered
Her modest face
So totally
Only last night,
Unhanging the lantern to reveal
Her beauty, and
Her rustic grace.

Among the Signs

You entrance me,
Hold me still, by the beauty
You present –
The cadence of your still small voice
Startling me
As your words wash me
Jordan-like in the midnight river

Night can be imagined to change into day, of course
As Dawn comes disguised
In Night's darkest robes
Soon tossed aside
Like you toss
Those tresses from your face

Among the signs
You are the memory
Of a song I knew long ago
Melodies reined in from the future

For you see far enough
Ahead
To caress
Each sigh found in
My careless life.

Virginia Slims

The dust is yet to be wiped from these shoes
The last journey still travels
Through my mind leaving
Mangled hearts
Broken dreams
Littering the track.

We have come a long way, baby.

Relay

How does one claim he travels light
When he travels with such a heavy heart?
Where do you put such a load?
Who will help us off-load?
Why should she?
The mind takes over from the heart.

Daily Resurrection

Like a dead lord lie I
Through the night
Still, naked and candid

But every new morning is the resurrection.
A voice whispers
"Let there be light."
I hear it
I rise.

The Play Goes On

Mid-motion freeze as lights dim –
An auditorium taut with bated breath
No sighs are heard
No smiles are sin.

In this vacuum where angels and ogres
Find reason

Zombies in the audience begin to sway
To haunting melodies recollected
From another circle
Soundless footfalls echo within
Their dying minds
Reminders of who they should be
What they once were.

They are lost where they are found
Racking putrid brains anxiously
For the whereabouts of their coffins.

Suddenly

The air is rent with the cackle of short-circuiting wires
A motorcycle starts outside. Stalls. Stutters.
Stops.

Unannounced an actor steps on stage and nothing is the
same
Anymore.
A bewildered director screams "Cut! Cut!"
But the play goes on.
This is no more the play we paid for.

From the front row
I see life take over.

The actor slumps to the floor
In search of his mind
Believing it was where he left it.
The audience begins to cheer.
Loud and clear.

Out of the hollow darkness of the auditorium
Somebody in pyjamas hollers "Enough!"
But the play goes on.

Remembering Carmelita

We sat cross-legged
Shadows cast
By two empty spaces
On the bed
Musing in the eternity it took
To cast that spell.

In the rubble
A gem incomparable
Smiles
Feeling transported in discovery
Beside a still moon mirrored
In an unmoving pond

Finding there
That tragedies inhere
In the moving passage . . .

Shall we unfold, unfurl and rise?
Do you not see
The beckoning speck
Beyond those shades?

Stir me Carmelita
Rouse me from this murderous slumber
Dart my soul
With your quivering touch
My spirit shakes in trepidation
My faulty foundation collapses
My eyes cloud over
With need to see you
What succour, Carmelita

What succour can there be
For a head scorched incoherent
What solace
But in the temple
Between your valleys?

Touch me again
Make tremble like serendipity again
Split those embers for the new sacrifice:
It's getting hot in here.

A Sphinx's Guidance

Deep down these dire straits
A sphinx requires guidance
To the unholy spot
Its riddle was first posed.

And he hummed and he haa'd
And he hummed himself indistinguishable
From the cacophony of parrots
Fluttering overhead
Silent shadows on the eerie sands.
Which shall we ask first
For directions?
The day is closing in, Wanda —
We must decide . . .

The strait is crooked now
The sun burns too coldly
For our soles' delight
Or our sorrow's comfort

But it burns
Soon the sphinx shall disappear
To reappear
At the end of its riddle
And change
Our notions of fire.

Realization

Cocoons cave in at a call
Mute mountains melting
Without murmuring
Or recall.

Till they note
Their elements devote
Too much energy
To this inane trembling

So they erupt
Champagning spectacles of fire spewing
Madness as they erupt
Rushing, sloughing
Ossifying soon in
Another eternity
Away.

Friends of Nick

Do they know that Nick is dead,
These two dogs playing?
Do they miss that one of them
Who left unfinished what he was saying?

The curfew tolled the knell of parting day.

An Easter Poem

The darkness lightened
Overhead
Long-circling clouds dispersed
As my doubts burst
Breaking out
In tears of release.

The distance filled with roses
Echoes of triumphant songs

These were the first sacred moments
Of new birth I touched.

How shall I bless that sanctified day
When you arose
And comforted me,
When you my Redeemer arose
And comforted me?

Sears of Yesterday

Here beneath
The somnolent shelter of true love
I recall
Yesterday.

In the eyes of her encircling embrace
I find
The peace part of her
Seared through and through
By its transience and our loss of faith

Over there
By the waterside
With faceless shadows
I once conferred
Believing every lie they told me
In the pact of our nameless order

So now the first of us gathers
The broken remnants of dreams we shared
Gathers together
The morsels of a feast grown cold
Tears down together
The weary scarecrows of our dream's scaffoldings
On this deserted island.

Transition

Eyes luminiferous splinters of sun
Beak bold and beautiful
An eagle flaps softly across the skies
Into the never-never country beyond these mountains —

Flaps far away
Into the suns and regions beyond its furthest dreams

Where the day holds
Realities held by no day before it
And the meadow holds
The fate of eyrie-less eagles flapping southward
To the never-never country beyond this land

And of vacancies left behind
Old memories in mists, and crags
Of these same mountains.

I Feel Estranged From You

I feel estranged from you
Mountains and valleys
Removed from you
On this old bed

I feel how nice it would be
When those former pleasant courts are permanent

And your face drifts like a spectral criminal
In a dream of loud hallelujahs
Borne gently to me through this eternal sea.

The Serenity Was Strained Too Soon

The serenity was strained
Too soon
In the lifelong moments of departure
Through my sieves
Into the storehouse of my recollections.

And I can tell
That it is only by your dramatic return
That I can find that former peace again.

Sparks On the Inside

Sparks flying and cackling high up
On an electric pole

Yesterday I trod through
The familiar territory leading
To my soul
Where I saw

Sparks flying free in an electric cosmos
And I couldn't say
If sparks on the pole knew about
The sparking inside.

A Pointless Ritual

There is no sense
In performing these rituals indefinitely
Without thought to their inherent pointlessness.

They are surrogates that reinforce
The need for you to be physical.

The Cow and the Bull

He brought them together
The cow and the bull
Harnessed them
As only he could.

Persuaded them to brace
His unruly ways
With the cow's contentment,
Her stillness
With his mobility

It was a bull's eye.

For You These Days

I told you
These were not the beautiful days
I promised us
I said
These were not the days of our life
And only further on may we find them
I always loved the sea's crashing in laughter
Against the shore
Dizzying ozone in the atmosphere
As squealing children ran barefoot
On a deserted beach
We brought them to.

You told me
These were the harbingers of those days
And these too were their sentinels
You said
Each day of the world was a day of our life
And we had enough strength to keep it.
You always loved the setting sun
Slowly drifting to the deserted beach
The quiet serenade of a midair eagle
As wonder-struck children rose
On this mountain
We brought them to
You said
Each day in the world is a day of our life.

This Wilderness of Things

This wilderness of life
My hopes crops in fleecing fields
My fears net-like casts
On still pristine waters.

This wilderness of hopes
My terrors like nickels tosses
Into bony fingers
Of eager shadows sitting sombre
On still concrete sidewalks.

This wilderness of nets
Ensnares me in human webs
Entangling circles
Tenderly tripping me in loving lassos and
Rewrapping me in the old webs.

This wilderness of shadows
On sidewalks of darkling desires
Melts in screamed silences wafting
On the watery winds
Of their idle minds.

And the sullen hills suddenly bellow
With wind-tost rumours
From ear to scented ear
While cattle low below
The bypass
Beneath the gnarled prairies.

And can it be
That this wilderness that Dinos trod
Is become such wordlessness as this
A dry oasis I should call home?

The Devil

He knows it
He must depart
If resisted.

One moment alone

And he is up and about,
Whispering . . .
Next moment, if we resist him,
He is gone.

For Nora

The softness of this evening, Nora
Touched me deeply
As passion flowed
Like a wordless stream between
The disbelieving shores of our souls.

The softness is the substance
Broken dreams are made of, Nora
The tense calm before the storm
Abundance of rain that follows...

So, we must be careful this evening
As passion like a wordless stream
Flows between us.

Brandy Poetry

When I think of you
A fiery poetry courses like brandy
Through my veins

My eyes fill
My mind rests
In a surrounding warmth who woos
Your face
As it floats before mine.

When I see you again
It will course more fierily,
This brandy poetry.

Into You

I delved

After he had spoken
Finding meaning
In a thousand mid-air spaces of words he had spoken.

I soared

Through the feathery airiness of freedoms I found
Before my eyes
In the waiting arms
Of a Night turning cold and pacing
In my yard

I dissolved

Into you
The territory
Of my childhood fantasies
The awakening of my boyhood dreams

Into you
As you stared.

Furtively She Came, Like a Fowl, and Stood

Furtively she came,
Like a fowl, and stood
Listening;
Straining, silent, bucket in hand,
And peered . . .

One-legged for discovery, and craned
Her neck forward, dead silent, and peered . .
Furtively . . .
Heart in mouth

Furtively
She fills her bucket
With water
And struts past me . . .

Illusions

What is the structure of an illusion?
Is it big, or small?
Does it crouch, or stand tall?
Can an illusion blind you?
Or, placed beside passion, does it elope
Suddenly, with its own mirages?
What, do you say, is the structure of an illusion?

Dreams may concretize
Into visions for those who see them
We certainly may sleep with our eyes
Closed and dream
But leaving our hearts open,
We see.
Where do illusions come from?

Through Your Eyes

Through your eyes
I found
The narrow passage
Where dream-like
I gathered
Wool upon wool
To tread my way
Back to reality.

Through your eyes
I saw
The grand prairies
Of my childhood fantasies
Where childlike
I gazed
At wonders upon wonders
Unfolding in the distance

It is only through your eyes
That I see
Dreams become power,
Shadows flee

Only through them
That I see at all.

I Write at a Bad Time

I write at a bad time
I really should not
I stand on the brink of a dire decision
Wishing the world would sway with me
To anarchy and revolt
I write at a bad time.

How does one escape one's limbo?
Move?
They hang heavy
These webs, on my mind,
Pauline fetters fasten my soul
I write at a bad time.

I Do Not Stroll Alone

Gravel grates beneath my feet
Crunching quietly as I walk
Amid heartbeats and silent melodies
To which I sway alone till the dawn

I do not stroll alone
A believing dream walks with me,
Straying far and snatched
From the night that nursed it.

"Traveller," she says,
"Where are we going?"

"Where did we go?"

I turn to see
The dream speaking to me and bump
Into your face.

You Stir Me Daily

You stir me daily
Love me each hour

In your breath I catch
The first whispers of rain
In the heat

I lie in the grass
Fed by a flowing raven river
Led to the other side
Where you greet me

In raiment soft as a cloud
And walk me through the brooks
And bigger woods of your fantasies
On the other side.

Cocks on the Green

Unbidden again we come
To this altar still drenched
In blood of my many martyrs
Drenched
In the perspiration of their sacrifice
In this oven of a vapid imagination

Slim tracers zip past my gaze
Orbiting the ceiling

Making me recoil
As light disappears
To leave this decadent silence of caves
At whose entrance
Fires dance like entranced African maidens

To a tune lost in three trickles
Of a silent stalactite. One drop
And the fires fume baking
Consciousness unconscious

In this dreary dawn of songs
Our heavy day of narration
Cattle low below
As the sun rises
Following cocks on the green.

Stirrings

Trees in my mind shudder
In awe of these menacing monsters

Rooted to their spots
Watching, seldom comprehending,
Uncertain till. . .

A reminding wind arrives
To ruffle their hair
Playfully and sigh
Stirring them to song and incantation
In a tree and universal language
Men cannot see.

One Trip Less Without You

In the belly of another whale
Through drum-rolls in the skies

We sail

Onwards and beyond
Escaping seas in one trip less without you

In one thought less
That could have been you.

How Do You Feel?

When the day is done
And the sun settles on a lone horizon

How do you feel?

When the night comes calling
Skipping close and saying
I shall hide you, my dear
In the womb of my own
Dreams and desperate desires

How do you feel?

Last night was the child of my mother
The moon,
A glowing softness inching near
Would you were here to understand
This belated repentance.

How do you feel when time is no more?
When serenity slips through
Your careless fingers
Down
The labyrinths of an entirely different sound
Until the incessancy of lakes lapping shores
Kills the memory of your personal silence?
Now that it's all over,
How do you feel?

Lessons of Life

The magician looked away
As I asked
"What is the substance of magic, Sir?"

The priest would not say
What tremors took one
Before that holy throne of God

The Lecturer
Conceited caricature of magician and God
Knows not even nothing

Darkness falls
On everything we did in the day
Tomorrow morning
We return
To the cold shrines
Of these mute ancestors.

Mercy Memoirs

Chilly day.
Blue panorama
Skirting birds above

Below, the lush expanse
Sliced through by skirted birds
Doing penance. A pity.

Chilled spontaneity
Continuous sound –
Screeching birds, screaming girls.

The silence suddenly dies

A long forlorn death
Tumbling like an echo
In a tunnel
To an indeterminate end.

Identity

Experience
Final frontiers
Unpleasant cycles.

Could one be one thing one moment
Another thing another?

We feel privileged
Here we stand
Distance away from what
Our present could have been.

We are there
We bounce
Up and down
We swing
Side to side and do
Those ridiculous jigs.

But here we stand now. Calm
Located
In the anonymous swarm
Becoming at last
What we'd always been.

This Gift of Sight

I should love
This gift of sight.

Why shouldn't I love
This gift of sight?

Alone shrouded
By sounds
I cannot see

A door slams in my face.

Same Place Some Place

The drums throb
A matter of distance between
Here and there
Now and then
Have we advanced, retreated
Or stood still?

Jolly noise
Cacophony in concert
Lusty songs, suggestive gyrations
Frenzied beat, assault on senses

A concocted accusation?
Constant congratulation?

An ingenious indifference.
There we stand.
Away from them.

In the dim throes of their broken bacchanalia,
Accused
Congratulated,
Ignored.

If There Were a Way

If there were a way,
However perilous, of skipping tomorrow,
At this moment, I would take it
And bring myself
Face to face with that hour which alone holds you.

If there were a way,
However difficult, of saying all the futile things
In my heart tonight,
I would say them all now; and
Make myself
Purged of the pain of feeling so much; and

As I know
I have prayed with you,
So, please God, I will live with you
If there were a way
If only there were a way.

From Nick

All I ever wanted to do was to follow you
Everywhere
The simple wish of a dog.

Dogs were born free, you said
And everywhere
They are in chains

Your scents chained my senses
In all places
To a rude unaccustomed duty
So I ran
Blindly wagging
Happily

You would not turn to see
How faithfully I ran
While tires screeched on the road
Leaving me

Everywhere,
Nick.

Sudden Sight

The madness falls like soft
Scales from our eyes
Restoring a blank glaze

The thunder rolls like desperate drums
In our hair
Leaving us dumb, mute.

Lightning flashes
And cracks
Like a whip

Reviving pain of a memory
Four days old.

Tolling Across the Road

A cheer each year
The day draws closer and near

Not hope nor fear
Is resident here

In the brick-by-brick echo
Of a whispered hello

Perfect bells tolling in paradise. . .
Seas hastily departing
Too suddenly for comfort or cold
For grief.

Finality is the sound of those bells
Tolling
Always
Across the Road.

Still Yourself

In this corner of the bustle
Still yourself
And rest
Be quiet
And rest
For wild tempos are not for you

The madness is pretence
For those who will
Not still themselves
Or be quiet
And rest.

These Blows You Deal Me

These blows you deal me, Lord,
Are heavy
One after
The other
They land
Thick
Heavy
Thuds
To the head
Body
The mind
Lord!
They are heavy.

Yet I know
These to be the feathery
Caresses of concern
Bashes of your affection.

I accept these as a believing masochist.

Thump me some more.

Rejoicing

Blow horns
Ye trumpets echo
We rejoice this day
For the Lord's Name is Glory
And His will Magnificence.

Fold up, you oceans, and stack yourselves
Layer by layer
As the mountains remove
And pile
One upon another
A pillar worthy
To the God I sing of

These shall be signs
Of the mighty works
He has wrought this day.

Nsukka Skies

Stars sprawl above

These Nsukka skies
The dire dreams of our souls
God's most open promises
Certainties of tomorrow's suns
Memories of the rainbow

Yesterday.

Rafters and Beams

Through these delicate rafters of my mind
I see the moon sliced through
In the beams of Sol's coupling
On squeaky clouds
Early yesterday
In the other hemisphere.

For Someone in PH

Horizons beyond your planted feet
Valleys undulate into hills
Behind which rises
A large unsparing orb
First of a thousand stars.

Luminous Dreams

This luminous orb,
Times we played
In Dream's garden,
Engages me now —

Times
Whose nights and days
Grew
Large and unfrocked,
A miracle in our own backyard —

They engage me now.

Glad To Have Met You

You look uncertain but I'm
Glad to have met you
Even if it took so long
And the sun no longer laughs
From my heart.

Glad to notice
Your smile still points to heaven
Even if your feet
Sift sand on the shore.

It's a disappearing tomorrow
You are waiting on
You must get up and come with me, Wanda,

Before it's too dark.

On Time and Things

As we watched,
The years rolled on the languid river and plunged

Relentlessly into the sea

Slowly flowing to the next shore

Times passed
Sometimes creeping
Sometimes flying
The pearls we sold we are found re-buying

Sometimes I remember what it all was like . . .

Sometimes I forget.

A Sea Serenade

The sea greets the land
In a heartbroken gesture of abandon –
A happy, sloppy kiss.
Many are the years of loneliness flung
Into that ordinary moment,
Many the reminiscences of past similar times.

Her lust unsatisfied
Ageless longing unfilled
She recedes
To the deep mysteries of her queendom,
The silences of her sad peace . . .

Meanwhile

The land stands akimbo
Following her retreat with numerous thoughts
And uncountable memories,
The salt dimming his eyes.

Innocence and Guilt

The sweet child turned
Her clear light on my face
I stared back
For a while

And looked away

When I saw that thing in her eyes
I hastily looked away.

Mine on the Leaves

The sun sprinkles
Twinkling showers of diamonds
On leaves.
A blinking awakening is this,
The birth of a leaf-like chandelier.

For Lost Companions

We wait within walls
Of this crypt, now
Damp with dew and decay

Within this blank Saharan space
A camel comes
As I speak with you

Familiar Stranger
What did you say your name was?

Is it still the same?

Nigerian Faces

Nigerian faces
National disgraces
Motorcycles, cars
Angry screams and scars
Uniting in nothing
Delighting in looting . . .

Soon another buccaneer comes.

You

I shall record you for history
Posterity will lose its forgiving art
If this emotion passed
Without that record.

I shall tell of your peace
The mystery it unveiled for me
The splendour of dawn
Namelessness of every morn

With Liberty
I shall record these things.

Passage Me to Calmer Waters

And suddenly I woke up
And screamed
Into the dense void

I was blind, I could see
You opened my eyes
Grew my faith

When manhood oceans tossed me
You passaged me to calmer waters
Believing through
The raging torrent

Why, what a finicky thing is this valley
It grows into Hills.

For Andy

My blood rests manure now
My flesh is feed
For voracious maggots
Will you resurrect me someday?

Soon my eyes will be sunken
In their sockets, I know
My moustache peeled away
Nose vanish
Lips unrecognizable, snarling first
To be licked away
By those voracious maggots
I once feared

But I – Andy –
What will become of me?

The Land Loves the Sea

Like a zombie wading
The land treads water
Sinking fast
Shaken by the too-brief encounter

The land loves the sea –
It is a plain thing to see –
As he turns away in time
To greet the soft sunset in the hills,
Presenting to him
A ring washed ashore.

Unweje Rijo

A wail tolls
The last dance of a dear one departing
On wings of fresh sorrow

In the high Rijo silence that noon
A new emptiness is born.

On Ideas

The idea comes, skimpily clad.
Poetry clothes it –
Rich raiment of words which weave
Patches of skin sufficient to show
How beautiful and pure
It once was.

The Man from Three Worlds

"Hey, asshole! Why do you
Treat me that way? I'm a robot
Like you, got some fundamechanical rights, you know"

He passed him by
Without a sound,
Not a single beep.

Night Marauders

My lantern grows dim, flickers and dies
The rain tries keys in my locks
I start.

Insistent voices grow outside
The door shakes repeatedly
In a great commotion

I must rise, but
Ensnared
I do not move

I scream, but the scream caterwauls
Voicelessly back to me
A ghost with no name
Echo without a past.

Three straws and I break through
To the surface
Awaking
To melting marauders.

On Years and Lies

Years are the ultimate
Layers of our Illusion
The tragic solace of Futility
When illusion bonds with experience.

Calends are plastered lies, peeling
From Reality-as-we-know-it
Dreams planned—
Dreams of the grave, that is.

And we construct arches above
The solidities of lies
Place flesh and muscle on skeletons of time.
But, soon,
We lose even this slippery grip on things—
These solidities—
and become those skeletons ourselves.

Joy in this Pure State

Joy in this pure state is not rarefied
—Or rare

When joy is a jam
Jamming comprehension
Distilling doubts
Fencing fierce fears

Joy is a bearded uncle
To whom we take
One nightmare
In exchange for another.

Scenes Still Tug

Scenes still tug at my reins
I wonder how long
I must wait
For your promise
Of liberation
The open fields
Of freedom that are
Your wide embrace
My Lord.

You are able to deliver me
From these false desires
The snare of the fowler
And the noisome pestilence

Deliver me from myself
Let my joy be complete
Once again
In your open fields.

Grass on Sunday

The grass is greener on Sunday because
You look more carefully at the splendour
Of things impossible floating just outside your mind.

The Slip

The can dropped
From her grasp.

Straightening, she pulled
At it again
Straitened once more
To wrap her wrapper
Securely about
That incorrigible waist.

Up with her right hand
Her left outstretched for balance
And, wiggling,
She was gone.

I Shall Rise Swiftly, I Say

The cloud lifted at noon

The tabernacle and human temples
Drifted after it.

There I was
In the shower
Unaware of the righteous social movement
Bewitched by the charms of this
Lovely Moabitess
Nigerian Delilah
And left behind.

I shall run after the cloud till I find it
Cast her arms and amulets
From my necks
Her bracelets shall jangle no more
In my jungle.

I shall rise swiftly, I say,
To the cloud
And if it be by night
That I come into the camp,
Then
The fire dancing in its midst will comfort me.

Freezing Morning

The Harmattan is here
Cold, unfriendly this morning
A rare luxury it is
To laze on in snooze
Linger a little longer
On dreams I've dwelt on
And drifted from
A thousand times before.

You come readily to my mind
This morning
And I wonder
Are you alone this early morning
Or does somebody stir slowly
By your side?
Is it your bed
Or is it his?
Is there joy in your heart
This morning
Or some ache
You find you must hide?

The sun is brave this morning I tell you
Battling clouds
And the fog
And the cold
This cold will warm for us someday
We will never wake up alone,
Not in the mornings anymore.

It will be your bed
And it will be mine
With a wee cot
By the side.

Goodbye

Quiet woman.
Only my feet
Grate your secrets

This noon.

You let me be
As I slept
Till your oceans bridged
Our continents
And the flutist cried.

Your eyes mirror me, gypsy
And I could stay here forever
Breathing deep
This fragrance of fanciful locks
Feeding fat on the nectar you showed me

Till those drums
Those restless drums and trombones
Pound me again.

Flickering Goodbye

As the fire sighs in dying agony
A lone star peers
Down at the world
And I
Settled to smoke smouldering embers
On the Harmattan grass this scarce

It is chilly grown of late
The fleeing moon flickers goodbye
On the wooden garden gate.

As I invoke your memory
By the dancing shadows of this flame,
Slim Girl

The wind maintains its quiet fury
Sweeping dust and ash and holy smoke
In my face
Incensed by the obstacles
In this field of your new unity:
The tree behind me
The mound that marks you
And I
Held motionless by IT.

Nemesis

an angel implacable
tossed the land unstoppable
in the disappearing midnight of her rage
trailing tassel and scented woe
in hut of monarch and palace of page.

what commotion was Pharaoh's house
that day
as
her gossamer passage brush'd
his crown
and it crashed
down
     clat-

           ter-

                  ing
a-
     cross
        the courtyard
  to
          sink
         s
          l
         o
          w
          l
          y
        in the
        bog
        behind
but the ears of night were stopped
and there he stands

stupefied
drenched
in the tradition of rains which began last night
and as the wind blows
he withers like herb
leaving only
ashes behind.

Corpses' Motorcade

They shatter our peace this noon
Sirens of power
Wailing
The pretence of corpses in cars.

A shatter of screams
Careens to the ground
Close to the thirsts of lining statues.

The head Zombie nods sagely
To the chaos
His governance brings
The head hearse carries
A sleeping star to the parade
Eyes closed
In the darkness of eternal shutters
Nose stopped
To the seduction of fawning perfumes
Ears blocked to the coyness of bleating wolves
A heart finally stilled
In the swirling abysmal void.

Farewell.

Disorientation Camp

Camp. Confinement. Crazy.
Going crazy. Feeling trapped. Parades and drills.
An inmate in a walled non-city
Walled in from without,
Walled out from within.
      Crisis . . .
      A crisis is on the way.
            Camp. Confinement. Going crazy.

A Nude Night

the streets spangle
with a thousand stars
crowded in the cowl of my walk
through neon lights

tonight we keep the rendezvous
with screaming sleepwalkers
and ghosts
in search of their tombs
when all bones are unearthed
against bleak curtains parting
a nude night.

we must keep this rendezvous
with quiet babies crawling
in search of their wombs
when mothers looked one last time at...
gomorrah, was it?

a sombre drizzle
washes the lights from my eyes
i see dancers in the distance

i must meet them and confess
i heard them
i tiptoed
on their hushed whispers
when they thought the whole world was away

and three little birds
betrayed their secrets
in the dawn.

Quaking Grass

as new rains fall
upon earth,
were we to bear
only presents and supplications, Dear Sovereign,
like mindless magi
had we done this with ease.

but, no.
we bear instead
our pasts and forsaken traditions
in this woeful receptacle
of an innocent sacrifice sought
in the deer leap of the next promise.

what difference had it made to you, Dread Sovereign,
if we had but come as usual
logging tomorrow in a casket and
prostrate spilt
her empty contents
at the feet of Your Majesty?

quaking grass
in the land trembles
in the wind of your passing stare
when all that ever stirred us
were dignity and bread, Sovereign.

So we said No.
We would bear none of these things
This time
But this morbid morsel of our decadent feast
Our best wishes to you, dead sovereign

A gift ript in the crib of nurture
Hollow-eyed staring at a future
So rudely
So suddenly
So ruefully sundered; and sad
As comfortless egyptians pleading
The life back
Into their limp firstborns.

Shadrach

Lately I have had Shadrach on my mind
Reflecting on reflections
Gathering in dancing flames
Stoked eternities ago.

Once there was a green field
On a hill
We sat on
In shades of pleasant memories

Confident

These passages
To secret plains and pastures would
Never be known
Never be thrown
Open to the scrutinizing skies
Of a cold criminal conspiracy

Confident

We leave for the stars
Following
That red-eyed moon like magi
Seeking
Absolution and
Blessings at Bethlehem
Certainty in certain places

Once there was a green tree
We befriended
In rare moments we pretended
It was Eden,
Berthing in the laps of Lemnos,
Believing we could
Drop anchor
Between Scylla and Charybdis.

But Eden brought us what
She wrought for us –
A thousand fruits
A thousand nights
A single flaming Excalibur

We descended
Into labyrinths of a promised furnace –
An inferno so steep it was no ordinary fire–
Singeing Nebuchadnezzar's godly goatee
As he flapped flames from his fanny and melted
Like the buttered ghost of a barbecued Babylonian

Heresy.

We sensed
From the edge
A figure in bigger flames
Dancing, prancing,
And knew
This was no ordinary fire at all
This was the Purifier

We ascended to greet Him
Good Meshach and I

Through thick smoke and fumes
To where they rose higher
And found
On a Rock
Scorched bread in one hand
Shadrach laughing at our surprise.

Adam Among the Rushes

Adam ran and hid
Naked.

Discovered
Obedience clothes us in righteousness.

Illumination

Here shielded
By your naked nearness
I look within
To see
What cup you hold

It is the clearest water
Gushing from the sides of a dying Lord.

A sanctified kindness
Is this cup you hold
My friend.

Drink it.

This White Fire

Again which cold,
Achi?
This fire sheathed in ash
Stifled within
The scabbard of its mute hearth?

Which cold did you say?
These soft flakes falling serenely,
As sighing leaves in Autumn?

But the cold is gone now,
Winter ended years ago;
The sun, lumbering, rises beyond
Horizons of our immediate dreams
Rising,
Smiling to tell us
Summer is near

To say
Closed vistas like flowers,
Pretty pupae,
Quietly,
Tremblingly, are opening.

In the space between our seconds
All ice melts
From the moments mounted
Above our minutes
Glacial lava comes rushing
Longing to fill
The false valleys of our apartness

Our hearts reach out
In space and time to pound
Their oneness and make
Sweet music of Earth's asymphonies
Led to and from lostness
By free songs in the skies
We find our way home
Meandering through
Labyrinthine lacerations left
By pain the cartographer
Hearing cheers in a full house of silence
Warmed through and through
By this white fire.

Birth of a South African Orphan

The elders of time are gathered tonight
Round Eternity's fire burning bright
Rallied together to know your score
Child don't panic, we've seen you before

Hooded eyes now darken and stare
Twitching noses sniffing the air
In a silence too silent for even thought
Foundation elders are casting their lot

The flames flicker as four elders yawn
Observing how soon it will be dawn
So, one more time a die is cast
This chance, they muse, will be your last

And in the early hours of the morning after
Dew trickles down the eaves and rafter
Through the tunnel linking here and there
You've come to us child, a new hope, a new fear.

The Mayor

The Mayor stepped down
To a calm applause
Like clouds in the wind-path
The crowds parted.

Quietly
They dispersed.

Down the road
Three shadows
Stood hooded conferring,
Menace hanging heavy
Like a nefarious necklace
On their conversation.

Quietly they melted
Into the dispersing crowd.

Next morning, the sun rose to spread
News of the Mayor's suicide.

Loneliness

The shower drips unexpected
Melodies like starting rain.

I am alone
In this shamble of dreams
Dresses, smells and echoes
Left behind
In departing footfalls
Of times and a people singing
The last songs
Of their identities

Soon all echoes cease
How long the interlude lasts
I cannot say, but
It must have been long enough
For the suspense to sag
Resistance give in

As the echoes begin
To drip again.

Noon Dreams

Beautiful dreams
Faded blue jeans with splitting seams. Carefree
In the open.

Sweet daydreams
Every noon seems flushed with moonbeams. Solitary
In the open.

Dreams, dreams. These mournfully sweet dreams
Like a mouthful of milk
And a bucket by the cow
Are all I have left.

On Silence

I seek absolute silence – an obsession I admit –
But where in the world may I find it?
There are always sounds in every silence
Always gods in the skies –
But I'm still searching.

A Reverie

As the last guest disappears through the gates
A playful wind settles lightly on the fronds
Swaying them
Jubilant thickets delay
Her diaphanous passage;
She presently pauses,
Light and heavyhearted
As on some long night
In a neglected, evocative spot
Quickened and rested
By unsilenced songs.

Stillness in the woods is our hymn this evening
As the sun slowly soaks the world
In darkness
Looking one last time at the befuddlement, his charge
From which Peace fled,
As she sank permanently into oblivion.

Jasmina appears.
Her voice leads me through those thickets
Into open places
Her hand in my ears gently guides me
To the present moment alone
And the confrontation
With those eyes which were speaking

Your house is quiet, she breaks into my thoughts
Her eyes mirroring
The dressed heavens
Their moon a black saucer sailing
Soundlessly through sea foam and oceans of my mind.

Shall we have music? she enquires
Her voice crisp and haunting in the gathering darkness,
The sudden sound of a ceaseless stream
Running beyond the caves of consciousness
And returning through underpassages
Into the same caverns again.

Taking her hand I say
No, not those wood-notes this time
Their sad ecstasy weaves
A crown of thorns and rests this on the roof
Marking this house out for the Lord.

A house strange enough
Sacred enough
Holy enough
For His repose and
Holy activity.

Beneath this roof we climb
Those spectral horses
Galloping through star-strewn alabaster skies
When hearts do not bleed
Nor tears metallic fall
On the corrugated safeties of our souls
Or, grim with rage, they buck us
And throw us
Light down
Crashing perspiring on beds below.

Spectral horses whose eyes blaze in awe
With will and power
On the track of no motion at all

Speechless
At the fickleness of their human riders.

Through these windows we see
Sprawling wonders of our landscapes within
Receding into far fields we never knew of -
Valleys and glades and hills -
In cool brooks of the meadows of life.

Beneath the waters, I lie and listen
Till I return, spluttering to the surface
For more carbon monoxide.

Untamed and self-revealed
I will stand naked in the sanctuary
Clothed only by temple fires
Burning about my scenes
While the windows wake to waves
Lapping against our shores
Wiping away yesterday's iniquity
Cleansing us from our scenes.

We step outside through the open door
This way
Into candle-lit chambers
Of secluded mansions of the soul
While walls within murmur
Unlocking calm secrets
As ceilings part to reveal
Celestial feasts of fire spread
In a moment the divine sparkled
With terrific tenderness of its own grace.
But. . .

Bold, impatient knuckles are knocking
Jasmina quickly departs.

The door clicks shut
To a hastily-flung farewell.
Loud voices clamber unto the sill.
The windows shut rapidly.
The feast is folded up
By corners of the sky...

As the first human guest appears
The ceiling falls into place.

Innocence's Viewpoint

He read her dread
It was plain to see
Fear scrawled on her faces

Her eyes were round
Big and afraid

He watched her sit, her legs weak
His beautiful eyes were watchful
As he sat in his cot
She looked away
Unable to face him.

He turned to see anger storm in through the door
Cross the room
Slam it shut.

She began to sob

Anger came out again,
Looked at her shaking shoulders,
The hatred burning in its eyes.
As the door slammed a third time
The baby finally began to cry.

Walk Blameless Before Me

You told me
To stand still,
I did.

You said
"Walk blameless before me"
I tried.

You reminded me of Jericho
Jordan
My wilderness
Red seas.

Horses and Chariots
Pharaoh's lies
Discomfited me.

This deliverance
Has no jubilation.
I failed you.

But I know you now
Faithfulness is your name
I shall put my trust in you always
Once this day of sorrow is done.

Take a Hike

The truck driver said
You should take a hike
And then he changed his mind (or
Did his mind change him?) and so
You hopped on, and
He hissed
And began
To vanish
Without you in him…

You really don't know how to take his silence
Do you?

It is oppressive
But you vanish anyways
With him
In him
Through him
In the tiny wisps of clouds locked so far away

You could never find your way back

Mirror Games

Take a look in the rear mirror
Come on
Take a look
Don't be afraid of what you won't find
Take a look, a real close one
Go ahead. Stare the mirror in the face
Outstare it if you can
Be very honest
Look in the mirror at yourself reflected in its eye
For a while…

And now tell me:
What don't you see?

He Spoke as the Clouds

He spoke as the clouds in a storm
So you can wait
Till it's calm and settled and peaceful again

Under the greenwood tree
He shall speak as the clouds
When the storm is over
And dawn's first rays
Leisurely wind their way
Across
The serene territories of your contemplation.

It will be over nearly as quickly as it began
And he shall smile calmly again

From behind
His formerly frightening countenance
He shall beam
Like the sun
From those same clouds which had
Thundered so fiercely
Merely moments before.

Gentle Night

The skies shake
Stars from their celestial robes —

Lonely and I freeze in awe, watching intently
As lamp-bearing angels commence
Their watch over you tonight.

Baby Talk

Two broken hearts mend together
Warbling through
Veiled meanings of babbling baby talk.

We can
Set foot firmly
On the draped mountains

We can
Reap in fields
Where we did sow

These two hearts
Broken in pieces.

We Will Let Our Blood Flow

We will
Let
Our blood
Flow,
Won't we?

Let more of it
Flow
In rage
Rushing to earth

We will let their blood flow
Won't we?
With this freshly split
Cake of woe?
This abandoned dread dagger?

See how limp the life force
That could have waved
To us tomorrow
See how dead it is
To these surroundings

Let these tears and blood
Mingle
In this okiki of mine
Mix them for a new hemlock
It shall be slow throes
No noble knows
A feeble stretch
And it's all haloes.

Lord of Nature

He thundered
In that terrible Voice of Authority
And sundered
Her womb's tranquility...

The baby crawled

Into the deeper recesses of its safety;
And there
He wondered.
And there
He cried.

One Moment

The drone behind.
The interminable denseness—
Trepidation lurking in hearts—
The intensity of Nothing-at-all
And the chiming clock
As her eyes found mine.

Home

Up the aisle
Destiny stands waiting
Before the altar.

The blazon of a cross
Up from behind.

Down that aisle
A forage through steppes
A race through prairies
On the way home
At last...

I Dreamed of a Candle Flickering Last Night

Down
In those depths where you determine Nothing
I dreamed
Of a candle flickering last night
It sputtered
And I saw
Strange images bearing
Strange messages rearing
Meanings striding naked in the light

I saw my serene sea-face paddled over
By limping shadows and gay gals
Mothered by a moon quivering cold
Across the still waters.

I dreamed
Of the loneliness within those shadows seeking
The essence of my sea-face
Seeking their substance in the moon's flattery
Designed on the brow of an ancient shipwreck…

Webs waft beneath my brow
I could dream no longer…
I strained to catch the last sounds
The paddlers were making

As their boat slowly sank
Beneath the still waters
The sun rose on the silence
And I saw
The candle was still.

His Touch Was Sacred to My Body

His touch was sacred to my body
As his words pierced
The sides of my ailing mind
Ministering healing there.

A Pleasant Lull

Harmattan
It's cold.

I've been indoors all morning
Thinking about things:
Hypotheses. Numbers. Grading systems.
The two "fields";
Catching myself thinking about
Thinking about these things.

How impossible it is to have time
And how impossible can come and take me.

Then I think that thought is not the best thing
At this time. I ought to go to school.
I will travel today. I ought to get up.

I start to rise, but sink back into the soft pillows.
A smile begins to greet me and I begin to greet it back.
Now we are both smiling,
This smile coming to my face
At the first thoughts of you
And the one coming out of it now.
It is time for my favourite thought.

Tribute to a Little Flower

Hey little flower
This is a tribute to your concealment.

I saw bougainvilleas once
Clinging to matter
Reaching out
Possessing space
Seeking more
Screaming "Hey! Look Baby!
"Amn't I beautiful!"
I saw that once.

I've seen glory and loss in my time.
In a rare moment an edelweiss
Pure, unstained, something rare
I have seen this too.

But I never saw you
Looking like this before
I never knew, never thought
Flowers had souls and could
Walk about.

Throes in the Deep

These throes circle long. Overhead.
They play pranks.
The applause dies too soon,
The dawn no different from the night.

Let us pray.
(To whom, sir?)
Let us pray to us.
Let us appeal to our tempers to restrain themselves.
Sizzle holy water on fiery coals.

I remember Christ at mass
Holding high His righteous chalice
Lucifer drowning in plenteous praise
His vile misbegotten malice
Did no angel see?

Was there night in Heaven dark enough
To shroud developing death
In this sacrilege of sacrifice?

Could angels sneak and plot
Within chambers of perpetual light
Without the knowledge of the Almighty?

Will those chambers be familiar again
When I get there?
Will I remember its breezes from the last time,
Savour another bath of divine refreshing winds?

I could stray ever onwards to the spiral's terminus. But
Do I want to?

I will be submerged
In its graceful waters, I can tell,
Pouring from the eternal throne
And live
In my grateful quarters
Forever adoring the Son.

Yakurr Retreat

On the crossroads to Convent, curiously
I miss the way
To Yakurr country —

Sokol where flows
Dread rivers in my veins,
Bleeding red vanities,
Livid as the rage that stains its history,
Past Soja Baal among yam mounds
Where madmen sacrificed mothers,
Buried alive and sprouting
Diseased pillars
To their deranged integrities

I wander far from the country,
As you can see,
To new-forming semblances of my soul
Where I discover
Several postmodernist souls at conflict,
War and peace
In the convoluting layouts of Yakurr science,
As far as I see, you see;

Which is why
You mirror me, 'Bcbe;
You salvage the terrific terrors I've told you still haunt
me,
and leave fragments of discarded souls
In Bikobiko beckoning
Through time,
Seeking

The repentance of warriors from other days,
Who bloodily hid their insanities
From rueful accolades they so stealthily sought,
So dementedly received.
I stray I say
Up from the bloody country
To the familiar shrines of clay deities
Wielding chaff staff and ruling
Mindless morons in their moon empires. Terrible.

They drip blood prematurely, these moons,
Their soils soiled
By reincarnations of crazed incantations—
Puerile profundities with only
A contrived relevance.

I suppose, then,
This totem pole is
The last phallic erection of their impotent morality.

Decadence of the wood it is carved on,
Sickness of the mind that skewed it, it points
To a sky darkened suddenly
By the evil it covers;

A sun no longer shining
A destination no longer there,
Yakurr stars are fading,
Falling silently from preordained perches,
Transforming into dreams untenable
A vain vision of valour in an empty night—
The quiet rebuke of Day.

Masindi

I'm tired of tiredness
Angry at anger
But who am I to say things
I know are never spoken

If I do not start now to contradict myself,
Lose myself so
I find myself, as I've said before,
In that endlessly gravelike quandary
That is
Just as still?

I Am the Fish Who Slipped Away

I am the fish who slipped away
Through your net,
Fisherman.

By prying through and thinking
It were better you wooed me and
Befriended me with the notoriety of your knowledge
And promised you'd be with me
When I fry.

I am the bird who got away
Through your snare,
Hunter.

But in courtesy I left floating
Down feathers about the fetters
You kept for my feet
Just so you know that feathers are free
And are of no use to you without spirit
Incompetent Birdman.

And I am the child who stayed
Mother
      In the discerning womb of your kind mercies
        Knowing that, knowing you, Mother
          You finally call all birds and fishes to you
            If they get away.